More Creative Dating

Contents

Acknowledgments

Should this book ever be used against us on the issue of our sanity, we would like to make it known that we were not solely responsible for its content. First at fault were our parents, Jim and Marge Fields and Cap and Joan Temple. They gave their approval to the concept in the same way they received our first crayon scribblings: "It's wonderful son . . . but what is it?" This book is the fruit of such unwarranted encouragement.

The information for the "I Love You" chapter was gathered by Marna Hillyard and Danielle Jullié. Marna's visits to the jungles of Mexico show what some are willing to do to see their names in print. As a consequence of asking dozens of foreigners how to say *I love you*, Danielle has received numerous marriage proposals.

Spencer Burke and Mark Clutter are to be blamed for some of the holiday ideas and a few others scattered throughout the book. Heaven help the women who have ever gone out with either of these men.

Other members of the guilty party include Mark Rayburn, who took our photograph for the first book and gave early inspiration to the project; Steve Titus, who taught our word processors to speak to each other (and helped us solve the ensuing arguments); and Russ Johnson, whose moral and financial support have increased our morals and our debt.

Our chief accomplice in this book is our partner, Steve Björkman. Steve's illustrations have brought life to ideas that had once been safely locked away in our minds. That makes him dangerous.

The contributions of others have been acknowledged following the dates they submitted. We have edited these ideas for style and grammar (we didn't want them to look better than our own), and have expanded them with our own material whenever we thought fit. There was no way to include all of the dates sent to us, and we appreciate all those who gave us their ideas for consideration.

THE "CREATIVE" AUTHORS OF THIS BOOK ....AND THE ILLUSTRATOR.

1.

Creative Ways to Ask Someone Out

To go on a date, you've first got to get one. And to get one, you've got to ask. Here's how to ask.

Free-Falling Bear

Pin a date invitation to a teddy bear, and set the bear on top of a slightly ajar door. Eventually, when she opens the door, the teddy bear will fall into her arms.
Note the following cautions:

A LITTLE TOO REAL, HUH?

- Avoid using live bears—many are scared of heights.
- Ceramic bears don't work either.
- Unless she wears a hard hat around the house, keep the overall weight of the bear to less than 10 percent of her own.

Bulletin Boldness

Find the bulletin board at his office and pin up a large date invitation. Even if he doesn't see it, he'll certainly *hear* about it from someone who does—he'll get the message either way. Keep an eye on a bulletin board near you for a reply. If he doesn't respond in three days, spray paint your invitation on his garage door.

Help with Dinner

Arrange for a delivery boy to be waiting with a prepaid pizza when your potential date arrives home to prepare dinner. As soon as she gets inside, the doorbell

I DON'T KNOW, LADY, I WAS JUST TOLD TO DELIVER DESSERT.

should signal another delivery: a bucket of fried chicken. Minutes later plan for the Chinese takeout to arrive. Just when she tries to figure out what to do with all the free food, you show up and ask if she's available for dinner.

Cover Girl

If you're ambitious and have some artistic talent, try creating a magazine cover featuring yourself. Get a good color photo enlarged to the size of a magazine cover, and use rub-on lettering to create graphics and article titles. Glue the new cover to an old magazine to give it the right feel. One of the article titles should be something like, "Cover Girl Julie Smith Wants to Date Russ Johnson . . . Will He Ask?" Other titles can read like the headlines on supermarket tabloids: "Monkey Gives Birth to Reincarnated Elvis Presley," "Cosmonauts Perform Head Transplant in Orbit," "Kitten Drags 12 People out of Burning Building."

Ms. X

It's Monday morning, and he's at the office. At 10:00 a Federal Express package arrives with an anonymous invitation to a play on Friday. At 10:05 a courier ser-

vice drops off one ticket to the show. By 10:15 the tux-edo shop has called for his measurements and told him when he can pick up his prepaid rental.

At 10:30 Western Union delivers a telegram telling him when to be ready on Friday; minutes later the lim-ousine company calls to verify his home address. By 11:00 the restaurant phones him to confirm the dinner reservations, and the florist calls to tell him the cor-sage and boutonniere will be ready for pickup on his way home from work Friday. At 11:15 the UPS driver drops off a package containing the theater program.

The noon mail includes an unsigned letter from you saying that you are looking forward to your evening together and that you want him to confirm plans by leaving the program on his car's dashboard when he parks at the office on Tuesday. The unsigned notes he receives on each of the next four days take his anticipa-tion to the limit.

If he is someone you know of through a friend or business associate but who doesn't know you, make the mystery last even longer by arranging to be picked up first and dropped off last. After arriving at his house, have the chauffeur escort him to the car. He in-troduces you as *Madam*, and explains that this is how you wish to be addressed.

If the date goes as planned and you wish to see him again, send another unsigned letter, to arrive on Mon-day, requesting the pleasure of his company again. Tell him you will reveal your identity if you are treated to a creative date of his own invention. You will know you have impressed him if you discover a private investiga-tor tailing you during the week.

Music Video

With professional athletes now making music videos, the way has been cleared for the musically ig-norant to use this art form in communicating. Send your prospective date an unlabeled video in the mail. When he hurries to view it, he'll hear a familiar song and see you appear on screen, mouthing the words. If you have access to two VCRs and an edit controller, you can recut an existing music video. When the camera switches to the lead singer, the sound is hers but the shot is of you—in costume and lip-syncing the lyrics. After the song, record a short message explaining that he was the inspiration for your performance. Conclude the tape by inviting him to your upcoming concert.

Engine Trouble

Open the hood of your prospect's car, remove the distributor cap,* and set it next to the distributor. Leave a note under the hood telling him that a skilled mechanic would like to share some "shop time" with him at his earliest convenience. Tell him to signal an answer: "Honk if it's yes; leave skid marks if you can't tonight but would like to get together another time; crash into the nearest tree if you never want to see me."

AT LEAST THEY LEFT A NOTE

---

*If you can't find the distributor, pull out the whole engine. Make sure to leave a longer note so he won't notice it's gone.

Kisses Defined

Peaches: When you say the word *peaches,* your lips come together for less than a second. Imagine saying this when you kiss—it happens very quickly.

Prunes: Described as such because the movement of the lips during this kiss roughly approximates that caused by uttering the word *prunes.* It's longer than a peaches kiss.

Alfalfa: Hold your tongue with your fingers and try to say *alfalfa*—you can't do it. Nor can you perform the alfalfa kiss without using the tongue.

Glass: This kiss is most commonly used when you are separated by a pane of glass. Oftentimes you are in a hurry and can't roll down the car window, or the sliding door is shut and you don't want to let the cold air in the house. If you are participating in a glass kiss and the other person pulls away to see your pressed lips, blow air into the window and make your cheeks swell.

Underwater: Remember wondering what it would be like to kiss underwater? Then when you convinced your neighbor to try it with you in the pool, you found out it was no big deal: you can't feel their lips very well, the chlorine hurts your eyes, and you swallow water on your way to the surface. It may be more interesting if you fill the pool with Jell-O.

Noisy: A kiss that makes noise is not unusual, it's just noisy—which at times can be considered rude.

Thrown: Not too common anymore. Seen mostly in parades and silent movies. Can be traumatic if you don't warm up your arm.

Blown: Similar to the thrown kiss, but used at close range or when a thrown kiss might be intercepted.

Hand: This kiss is another member of the thrown-kiss family. The only difference is that after the kiss is placed in the hand, it is personally delivered and applied to the other person's face. Although more accurate than either the thrown or blown kiss, it can be hazardous if delivered with a slap.

Dark: Kissing in the dark is a problem for those with bad sense of direction—they end up kissing the ear. One way to alleviate this problem is to locate your date's nose, grip it tightly to use as a reference point, and kiss just below the hand.

DAVID........YOU JUST KISSED MY NOSTRIL.

Grandma Bunny: These are the types of kisses you get from older relatives. "Bunny" refers to the soft white hair grandmothers have above their lips, which they often moisten before kissing.

Self-Disclosure

Send a package to your prospect. Tuck this message inside: "I can't expect you to go out with me until you know a little about me." Fill the box with gifts and notes that reveal your character:

- A tape of your favorite music: "I have good taste."
- A cartoon book: "I have a sense of humor."
- A copy of *War and Peace:* "I'm well-read."
- A photo: "I'm better looking than my dog."
- A package of confetti, streamers, and party whistles: "I know how to have a good time."
- A bag of chocolate kisses: "My weakness is chocolate and kisses."
- A map to your house and tickets to a show: "I'm generous, and free next week to go to the show with someone who wants to find out more."

Table Talk

Some restaurants set plastic mini-displays on the tables to point out dining specials. Find out where your prospect will be eating lunch (you're going to have to do this on your own—we don't have *all* the ideas). Ask the hostess if you can slip your date invitation into the display on the table where he'll be sitting. Calligraphy or professional typesetting can help your invitation catch his eye sometime during the meal. If he misses the trick all together, don't despair—the next guy to sit at the table may be a better pick.

Video Dating Service

The age of video has spawned a new generation of dating services. Members of the service can watch videotaped interviews of prospects and then decide which persons they would like to date. Here's how you can create a dating service video of your own.

fountain pen, write an invitation to your prospective date. Fold the paper and close it with a personal wax seal.

Recruit a friend to act as page. He should dress sharply and be versed in all the appropriate manners of a page. These include bowing to the lady when entering and leaving her presence and addressing her in the third person (e.g., "The gentleman cordially re-

THE OUTCOME: Woody's cute neighbor moved within the month; her cat is deaf in one ear. Woody now recognizes that there is a fine line between creativity and malicious behavior. He continues to cross over that line, however, and has numerous lawsuits pending against him. Sorry, Woody.

—Bruce Cavers, *Anaheim, California*

quests that the lady make reply forthwith to the gentleman's invitation"). The page arrives at her house, delivers the letter, and waits for a reply. The page furnishes her with pen, paper, wax, and seal. When the page returns with her reply, quickly respond with a note. Have your page deliver this with a bouquet of flowers or rotten eggs, depending on her answer.

Bedtime Story

Invent your own fairy tale. Write it out on pieces of parchment, draw illustrations, and bind the pages together with gold yarn. Make arrangements with his roommate to visit your prospective date just as he is about to fall asleep. Sit by his bed and read him the story—be sure to show him the pictures in case any of the words confuse him. Leave the storybook with him when you go. The story can go something like this:

Once upon a time there lived a lovely princess who liked the handsome prince that lived in the next kingdom. Though the prince knew of her, he was a shy prince, indeed, and did not seek her out. Now the princess was not shy, and she set out to arrange a date with him. The easiest thing to do would have been to send him a message requesting that he escort her to one of the many royal functions that she, being of royalty, was required to attend.

But the problem was this: In the kingdom of the prince, the custom was that men sought out women—for women to seek out men was wrong. So the princess, being a smart cookie, devised a plan. She entered the prince's castle disguised as his royal storyteller and went into the prince's chamber. She knew the prince was accustomed to hearing bedtime stories. The story she read to him was about a brave young man who had a prophetic dream. As her story went, this young man dreamt that the next day there was to be a royal picnic in the palace gardens of the next kingdom. At this picnic, he would meet a princess who would make him laugh and serve him wonderful food and drink. Well, the story that our smart little princess told was so long that the shy prince fell asleep and awoke the next morning sure as a sandpiper that *he* had the dream! The shy prince arrived in the palace gardens the next day at noon—the customary time of all such picnics. But to his surprise, what should he find but that there was no royal picnic—just a beautiful princess and some wonderful food and drink. It was not long before the shy prince was filled with laughter—to say nothing of fine food and drink—and was quite pleased to be the only guest.

The day after you read him the story, plan on having a shy prince come to visit you in your own garden. If he doesn't show up, send some knights back to his house to burn it down.

2.

Cheap Dates

You don't have to be poor to be a cheap dater—just willing to invest more creativity than money into a date. And if you don't know how to date without lots of money, this chapter can save you a few bucks.

Dating Ideas Booth

Set up a booth with a sign that reads DATING IDEAS BOUGHT, SOLD & TRADED. Some of your customers will have great dating ideas they would like to sell or trade. Others will be looking for dating ideas they can use that night, and some will be desperate enough to pay inordinate amounts of money for a hot idea. Write down the dates that people sell you so you can turn around and sell them to someone else. After a few hours, the two of you should shut down the booth and take the most creative idea you collected for a test drive.

NOTE: If you encounter one of these booths on a college campus, be aware that prices for date ideas tend to be related to the majors of the students running the booth. For example, *social science* majors tend to charge low prices and even give away some ideas to those in need; *pre-law* students sell the date ideas at an honest price but make you sign a release of liability statement in case you get stood up; *engineering* majors design impressive booths, but they take so long to build that they're not ready to open until summer; *economics* students sell date ideas for about 10 percent more than they paid for them—and get field-study credit for doing it; *business* majors mark up the ideas a full 50 percent and then send them to us in pursuit of even more profits; *English* students just sit at home waiting for the business majors to send in their ideas—then they turn around, write a book with the ideas, and retire on royalties.

Bathroom Date

After five on a Friday, most offices are deserted—and so are the building's rest rooms. Ask your date to pick you up at the office, tell him you'd like to treat him to dinner at a very intimate little place you know of. When he arrives, tell him to wash up in the men's room. Here is what he finds inside:

The lights are out, and candles are flickering in the mirrors. Violin music is playing from a portable stereo balanced on the urinal. A table in the middle of the floor is set with linens, china, crystal, and silver. The meal courses are on trays arranged across the counter, and the drinks are on ice in a bucket in the toilet.

—Kathleen Weyhrauch, *Eden Prairie, Minnesota*

Corner Portrait

For this date you'll need an easel, art pad, paints, and brushes—and no artistic talent. Set up your easel on a crowded street corner and have your date strike a pose nearby. If you have no aptitude for this, your painting will declare that fact soon after you begin. That's why you must play the part of a serious artist and pretend you know precisely what you're doing. As you get into it, people will stop to look at your progress. Some will laugh. Others will glance from the paper, to the model, to you, and then back to the paper. Then they'll wrinkle their foreheads and scrunch up their eyes, and still not get it. Turn to these folks and ask questions like, "A little more blue in the hair, don't you think?" And there will be a few (very few) who really admire your work—these people are dangerously sick. When you've finished the portrait (or attracted such a crowd that you can't see your date anymore) change corners, swap places with your model, and do it again.

Crayon Portraits

Set up your easel on a crowded street as you did before, but hang a sign on the back that says CRAYON POR-TRAITS: $1.00. Your date can be your first customer. While he sits on the stool next to the easel, you sketch his portrait in crayon. If you're really bad, you can entertain a crowd and drum up some business at the same time.

Chez McDonald's

Tell your date to wear her nicest outfit—you're going to take her to the best restaurant in town. Have a friend act as chauffeur and drive you there. Walk in the entrance, go straight through the kitchen, and head out the back door. Now get back in the car and drive to McDonald's. Have your "chauffeur" go in first and set a table with linens, china, crystal, silver, candles, and flowers. He then brings you inside to be seated. The menu has the entire selection written out elegantly, le gran mac, les potages français, le Coke, and so on. He takes your order to the counter and pays for it. When the food is ready, he removes it from the plastic and paper and serves it on the china and crystal.

—Michelle Smith, *Colorado Springs, Colorado*

Product Testing

Why is it that actors get to do all the testing for products we see advertised on television? They have lots of fun ruining blouses, destroying cars, and staining carpets to prove their products are better than the rest. But they don't have to be the only ones who have to have all of the fun—you and your date can test these same products to be certain that the commercials are true. Does that driveway spot-remover really remove oil spots? Find the company owner's house and use his product to clean up the oil you spill on his driveway (that's credibility). Does that detergent really get out the tough stains? Wear white outfits to an Italian restaurant and spill spaghetti sauce and salad oil on yourselves. If the detergent gets the stains out, send in a testimonial—you may land a contract for a commercial. If it doesn't get out the stains, send the manufacturer a bill for the new clothes you buy—and send the results of your test to the company's competitors.

Back to School

Take your date to his old high-school or junior-high campus for a glimpse at his past (if you're ready for what you may find). Have him show you his old locker,

favorite instructors' classrooms, and where each clique hung out. Bring along an old yearbook to browse through and further trigger his memory. If he appeared in any candid photos taken on campus, have him reenact the shot while you record it on film. Afterward, ask for a tour of the neighborhood. You'll want to see where he worked, where his friends lived, and where the local hangouts were. Visit an old girlfriend and find out why she dumped him.

Child Photographer

Many malls and department stores have portrait studios that specialize in photographing children. Although it is fun to watch a smartly-dressed toddler pull the background curtain down on top of himself as he drools on the photographer's light meter, the real entertainers are the parents trying to get their kids to smile.

What To Say To Ensure a Lousy First Impression

- Are you my date?
- Can we hurry to the car—I don't want my neighbors to see me with you.

WHAT WAS YOUR NAME AGAIN?

- I've got to be back in thirty minutes.
- Are any of your friends cute?
- Please don't talk to me tonight.
- Do you promise not to tell anyone I went out with you?
- Can I just have the money you plan to spend so I can go out by myself?
- Wouldn't you rather just talk on the phone?
- I'll be honest with you. I think you're a geek.
- Would you mind if I rode in the back?
- Don't get any ideas about touching me tonight.
- Can I follow you in a cab?
- Did you actually pay money for those clothes?
- Why do I always get set up with people like you?

- Can we sit at different tables tonight?
- Do you mind if I bring this small bag? I'm feeling kind of sick.
- How much money do you have?
- Who was president the last time you dated?
- Can we hurry and get this over with?
- Don't bother meeting my parents.
- Is that a whitehead on your lip or didn't you wash your face?

- Can we go someplace loud so I don't have to talk to you?
- Are your parents proud of you?
- Is it true that your nickname is "dime a dozen"?
- That's the biggest zit I've ever seen.

You'll see dancing, singing, whistling, puppets, toys, distorted faces, bribes, and threats. When that gets old, watch the photographer stare at this ridiculous behavior. Most children's photographers have a few tricks of their own. After learning the photographer's repertoire, make guesses with your date on which trick will work for each kid. Will it be the red clown's nose, the monkey face, or the lens-cleaning tissues stuck in his ears?

—Polly Averyt, *Huntington Beach, California*

Job Date

Send your date a memo asking him to come to your place of employment. When he enters your office, ask him to get something out of your bottom file drawer, in which you've hidden a sandwich and a canned drink. Hand him a golf putter and ask him to hit his drink into the conference room. Eat lunch at the table while your boss plays waiter.

Cheap Yachting

Start by going to a department or sporting-goods store to shop for your vessel. Buy the inflatable boat of your choice—$20 will get you a beauty. Make sure you

have paddles and life preservers (the flare gun and radar aren't necessary). Before launching your pleasure craft in a nearby pond, you may want to name and christen it. Seasoned sailors will tell you to put the name on with felt pen rather than carving it into the hull, and the yacht will be more seaworthy if you pour the champagne across the deck instead of breaking its bottle on the bow.

After putting out from shore, serve a light meal—the size of your boat will determine how light. CAUTION: don't try to cook on board. The smell of burning rubber will wreck the mood.

Other on-board activities: troll for shark; paddle in circles while eating lime Jell-O—see who turns green first; play backgammon, checkers, or horseshoes; watch for shooting stars; train dolphins; read *Moby Dick* or *Jaws;* and if you disregarded the warning about cooking on board, have a contest to see who can bail faster.

Helpful Nautical Terms

- *port*   left
- *starboard*   right
- *bow*   front
- *stern*   back
- *square porthole*   the hibachi-shaped hole in the bottom of a rubber boat

- *anchor down*   warning shouted from freighter dropping a 5000-pound anchor
- *Dramamine*   what winners take before the Jell-O competition

Toss of a Coin

Go on a drive to the city. Each time you come to a red light, flip a coin: heads you go straight, tails you turn (flip it again to find out which way to turn). Have your coin make other important decisions: Should I honk at this person? Should we stop and buy a diamond necklace at this jewelry store? Should we eat ice cream from this shop? Should we get out and run around the car at the next light? Should I swerve at that person who just littered?

—Suzi Qvistgaard, *Newport Beach, California*

Ugly Restaurant Contest

Restaurants pride themselves on their interior design. Some, however, deserve an Ugly Restaurant Award. You and your date can visit various eating establishments in search of the town's ugliest. Neither your wallet nor your stomach can survive a meal with every inspection, so just peek at each candidate briefly and then move on until you find the winner. Don't choose the winner simply because it's plain; the winner must look as bad as it does because somebody actually thought it looked nice that way. You don't need to present an award to the owner, but you should sit and eat.

NOTE: This date can be a good way of discovering your partner's tastes; if he or she adores the decor you selected as the ugliest, then you'll know whom not to ask for help when you're thinking of redecorating.

Thrift Store Wardrobe

Make plans to attend an event that you and your date would ordinarily never go to. Depending on your age and lifestyle, this could be a punk-rock concert, bingo night, roller derby, high-school basketball game, harpsichord recital, or reptile owners' exhibition. Now go to a thrift store and find outfits that will help you blend into the crowd. When you arrive at the occasion, make careful note of the language and behavior of the group and mimic it as well as you can. Your goal is to be so typical that no one even knows you're there (at a punk concert or roller derby this will also give you the greatest chance of survival). You may learn that this new crowd fits the two of you better than the folks you usually hang out with. If so, go back to the thrift store and exchange the rest of your wardrobes.

Here are some tips to help you fit in at some of the more common events:

Punk-rock concert. Put mashed potatoes in your hair, and then take a nap. Go to the concert the moment you wake up.

Roller derby. Ride a motorcyle to the arena, and put on your makeup when you get to 60 mph. Root for the home team or die.

Reptile owner's exhibition. Leave the price tags on whatever you wear.

Blind Switch

This idea will help you start off your next blind date with a twist. Roger arrives to pick you up. You hide in another room and send your roommate to the door, answering to your first name. She is wearing curlers under a scarf, a smudge of cold cream on her cheek, and cat hair all over her clothes. She invites your date in and serves him something to drink. After spilling the drinks and tripping on the carpet, she sits down to chat. Roger has a hard time concentrating—he's too

busy hating himself for agreeing to a blind date. When you see him staring at the window looking like he's pondering a jump-and-run exit, walk out and introduce yourself: "Hi Roger, I'm Carol. Sorry I'm a little

late getting ready . . . I see you've already met my roommate Carol. Well, shall we go?"
—Ruth H. Beloungy, *Prairie du Sac, Wisconsin*

Double Blind Switch

You and a male friend can use a variation of Blind Switch to arrange a date for your roommate. Set it up like the first idea, telling her that you have a blind date with a guy named Roger. Only this time the guy who shows up at your house looks and acts like a nerd. While she begins to feel sorry for you because you have to go out with him, there's another knock at the door—it's the *real* Roger (your friend). "Hi, Carol, *I'm* Roger—this is actually my buddy George. I asked him to show up and act like a nerd to play a joke on you . . . was it funny?"

While your roommate is wondering what has happened, you walk out bewildered. "Hello, I'm Carol . . . which one of you is Roger?"

"I'm Roger, but I thought *she* was Carol."

"She's Carol too; we're both Carol, but I'm the one you're going out with. But wait a minute; if you're Roger, then who is this?"

Roger smiles sheepishly and answers: "This is my friend George. He came here pretending to be me, thinking that your roommate was my date . . . this is very confusing!"

Now it's your turn to confess. "Well, don't feel too bad—her name really isn't Carol. This is Maureen, and we tried to play the same trick on you!"

If George and Maureen don't suspect anything by now, then you and Roger are either great actors or have stupid friends. Whether they catch on or not doesn't matter; the important thing is that they agree that a double-date will begin as soon as Maureen can get rid of the cat hair and George wipes the toothpaste from his chin.

Changing the Rules

Sometimes being creative means taking a normal activity and adding a little bit of the unusual. Here's a date that does that well. Instead of going to dinner, play baseball—on a golf course. Change the rules of the game to match the setting: hits into the sand traps and roughs are fair; the fairways are foul territory. Use a golf ball for the baseball and a tennis racquet for the bat. When the sun sets (or when you get kicked off the course) retire to a park bench and play board games under the light of a kerosene lantern. Play Monopoly according to your own rules. When passing GO, pocket $1000 instead of $200. If you land on someone's property by rolling doubles, that person has to give it to you, but you lose a turn. If it looks like you're about to lose, switch to Scrabble. If you can talk about a made-up word for 30 seconds without laughing, you can count it. When it starts to get late, give your date a goodnight kiss on the elbow—then throw shoes at each other.

BUT OFFICER! WE WERE JUST CHANGING THE RULES!

Food for Thought

Take your date to a supermarket to buy the appetizer, main course, and dessert for that night's dinner. Once in the store, go shopping in separate directions. Your goal is to try to guess what your date will choose and then pick the complementing item. For example, you choose lettuce and he buys salad dressing; you select noodles and he picks sauce. But when you both come back with cake mix and no frosting, you've got a start over. If you finish before the store closes, walk to different cars, drive to different houses, then eat your meal together.

Yogurt Tasting*

Your mission: find the best-tasting frozen yogurt in your area. To keep this date cheap, don't *buy* the yogurt—just *taste* a sample from each shop. When you've decided on a winner, go back and order.

Baby Face Slide Show

Round up slides of you and your date when you were babies. Put together a slide show using nursery songs

---

*This date works best for those who have no class and receive a great deal of joy from making others mad. It also works okay if you are about to move out of town.

as background music. Be careful about what you laugh at—women are hypersensitive to words like *chubby, ugly,* and *hairy.* (If she mentions any of these words, stick a pacifier in her mouth.) During the show you should serve drinks in baby bottles and eat Gerber mashed peas.

Impromptu Scavenger Hunt

For a cheap meal, make up your own scavenger hunt on the spot. Take a stroll around the block during dinner hours. Using your noses, try to guess what each household is serving. Make out a list of some of those foods that you feel like having for dinner yourselves, then start knocking on doors. When they answer, tell them that the two of you are on a scavenger hunt (you *are* scavenging for food) and show them the list of things you're trying to find:

> *1 swordfish steak, medium rare*
> *2 servings of potato salad*
> *4 hot biscuits, buttered*
> *2 ginger ales*
> *1 banana*
> *8 cookies*
> *2 sets of plastic eating utensils and napkins*
> *1 candle*
> *1 handful of after-dinner mints*

When you've gathered enough food to serve dinner for two, head home and eat up.

Airport Addition

Have dinner at an airport cafeteria. After filling your meal trays, try to guess the other person's total bill—loser pays for both. *A note to the naive:* When calculating the total, pretend the food has been flown in

Creative Dining Spots

restaurant parking lot
subway
storage garage
furniture store
island on a boulevard
cornfield
rest stop

top of a hardware store
balcony
middle of a football field
oil derrick
under an overpass
over an underpass

golf course
parking complex (top level)
gas station
top of a station wagon
fire engine
tree house
traffic school
end of a pier
plant nursery

empty pool
cave
drainage ditch
forest
roof of a house
suspended from an engine pull
laundromat
police station
radio tower
inside a dumpster

from the finest restaurant in Paris; now add $100 to the price and you should be in the right ballpark. *A note to anyone making less than $50,000 a year:* Skip this idea. *A note to anyone making more than $50,000 a year:* Call your insurance company to see if food poisoning is covered under your plan. *A note to airport cafeteria owners:* The price on this book was misprinted—please send us the balance of $54.00.

Free Limousine

Take your date to a limousine service's parking lot. Ask someone if you can look inside a few of the cars to see which one you prefer. When you find one you like, get inside and lock the doors. Now break out the drinks and hors d'oeuvres hidden in your trench coat, and see if you can catch a movie on the tv before the owners come with the key to get you out. If they can't unlock the doors, they may rock the car to disrupt the television reception. If this should happen to you, play it safe: buckle up.

Creative Influence

Now that you're such a creative dater, don't you feel sad for the many people whose dates are as dull, predictable, and lifeless as yours once were. Do you sense a heartfelt desire to add dignity and worth to their social lives? If you are one of those rare individuals with a genuine burden for the dull daters in your community, we salute you. And we also have another date idea for you.

Working together, you and your date should come up with a page of simple, creative ideas. They should be inexpensive and based on things that can be done

right around town. Run off several copies of your list and hand them out to the "dating hopeless"—couples standing in the ticket line to see a movie or walking into the video rental store. If a couple crumples up the paper, say, "Hey, you boring people must have read the wrong side!" (or words to that effect). If a couple decides to step out of line and go do something creative, then congratulate yourselves—and take their places in line (since you're so creative, one dull and boring movie date might do you some good). By the way, owners of these establishments may not appreciate the bad press, so if your tires are slashed when it's time to go, just think of creative ways to get home.

3.

Childish Dates

Every once in a while it's fun and healthy to escape to childhood. Here are some ways to make that journey with your date.

Finger Painting

Buy several colors of water-based paint. Place a glob of color on paper and smear it around with your fingers. Make several pieces of art, and hang them out to dry. Be sure to give each other your best ones. When she hands you hers, say, "It's beautiful dear . . . um . . . ah . . . er . . . what is it?" Now accidentally start a paint fight: first spill yellow on her arm, then try to wipe it off with your blue hand; when she smears red onto your face, counter with purple polka dots on hers; then when she dumps the orange into your lap, pour

the green into her hair. Now spread butcher paper on the floor and roll around to make body paintings. Finally, hose each other off in the driveway to make a rainbow river.

Children's Stories

Read a classical children's story to each other. If the story is long, plan for several nights. Make the story into an adventure by dressing like the characters as you read your lines. Create the atmosphere of the story

with background music and oil lamps. If you can, read the story "on location"—somewhere that fits the setting of the story. Here are some good stories to immerse yourselves in.

Robin Hood: Read in a very dense forest, wear green hose, carry bows, and give a gold arrow pin to Marion.

The Call of the Wild: Pick a snowy night to read together. At just the right moment, have a pack of wild dogs run in to greet you.

Treasure Island: Sit at a wharf or near a marina; copy the map in the book onto parchment paper so you can follow along as you read. Fill your date's pockets with gold coins.

Rinkitink in Oz: Read on a beach or in a boat. Bring a silk bag with three pearls in it—a blue one, a red one, and a white one.

Play-Doh

Pick up an assortment of colors at a toy store. Mold different colors together to make imitation hors d'oeuvres—give these to roommates to test the quality of your counterfeiting. When you tire of this childishness, let your date know by squashing whatever it is she is working on.

Jump Rope

Take a 12-foot piece of rope to a park on a Saturday afternoon. Tie one end to a tree, about four feet off the ground. While one of you swings the rope in large circles, the other jumps into the action. If there are children nearby, encourage them to join in.

Some jumping tricks you may wish to try:

- Do tandem jumps with your date while someone else swings the rope.
- See how many children can jump simultaneously.

Avoiding Embarrassment

In dating there is one thing you can count on: sooner or later, you're going to find yourself in an extremely embarrassing predicament. Here are a couple of common causes of dating humiliation, along with practical solutions that may keep you from being discovered as the klutz you really are.

Burps, Stomach Growls, and Worse

Symptoms: Loud gurgling sounds, strange looks from your date.

Diagnosis: If you felt it, you've got it.

Treatment: The noises themselves are difficult to stop. The best thing to do is try to mask the sounds with other noise. Vinyl seats, Naugahyde restaurant booths, and other common surfaces

UH....I JUST THOUGHT I'D OPEN THE WINDOWS FOR SOME FRESH AIR...

can be rubbed or hit to imitate a sound your body has made, making it difficult for your date to convict you of the offense. Discovering a sound that is close to the original is important since it is likely that whatever caused your body to emit the noise may very well encourage it to repeat the utterance—body noises seem to travel in packs. If the noise cannot be replicated, try concealing further outbursts with loud sound. Turn up the car radio or go to the drag races.

Body Odor

Symptoms: Suspect this problem if your date refuses to sit next to you in the theater, insists on taking separate cars, or avoids being downwind of you at any time.

Diagnosis: To discreetly investigate the scent emanating from your underarms, try this. Scratch your right shoulder with your left hand and look over your left shoulder at the same time. This exercise will put your nose extremely close to the suspected source of the problem—a quick sniff can give you the answer. If you discover no unpleasant odor, repeat the movement with your other arm (this test does not work if you have a cold).

Treatment: While shopping, insist on visiting the fragrance counter of a department store; sample as many as you need to overpower your own fragrance. In a restaurant, feed your date spicy food—this causes the sinuses to run, blocking the sense of smell.

- Set up another rope to swing in the same place, in the opposite direction—try jumping both ropes.
- Try dribbling a basketball while jumping.
- Count the number of jumps someone can make without missing.
- Swing the rope faster and faster to see how quickly someone can jump.
- Tug hard at one end of the rope; when the person holding the other end pulls hard too, let go of the rope.

After a few minutes of jump rope, you will feel on the verge of collapsing—this is a normal adult response. Sit out a few rounds to sip lemonade and watch the children outjump you in every way.

Toy Planes

Pick up some cheap planes at a toy store. They are usually made of balsa wood, Styrofoam or plastic and cost as little as 25 cents apiece. Purchase a few of these aircraft and fly them at a park. Put together your airplanes and fly them in various competitions: long-distance, high-altitude, and stunts. (If your date's glider outperforms yours in all the events, step on it.) Find a high spot from which to throw your gliders—one person launches while the other retrieves. When you get tired of toy planes, dismantle the survivors and store them away for another day—or another date.

4.

Busting Shopping Date Boredom

Some people love to shop. And since these same people don't like to shop alone, they often drag others along just to keep them company. Have you ever been one of these tagalongs? Maybe you have wandered through department stores in desperation looking for something to entertain you while she tries on her seventeenth dress. We have developed a boredom-busting mind game that will keep you happy. The way it works is you roam through the store trying to imagine the most obnoxious thing you could do in each department. You never actually do any of it—just thinking about it can keep you entertained for hours.

Try to imagine yourself doing these stunts:

- *Full Volume:* Get cotton balls from the cosmetic department and stuff them in your ears. Now make your way to the home-entertainment department and casually crank up every tv to full volume. When salespeople from the entire store storm the department to shut off the sets, give the stereos a volume workout.
- *Hanger Swap:* Systematically remove all the socks from their little sock hangers and place them on the tie hangers. Now put all the ties on the sock hangers.

- **Mannequin Maneuvers:** See how many mannequins you can "adjust" before being asked to
  leave the store. Turn hands and heads around,
  place pencils in fingers. Switch wigs between
  mannequins (or shoppers). Hang underwear from
  ears and earrings from noses. Place a squirt gun
  in the hand and a stocking over the head—shout
  "Robber!"
- **Scent Test:** The fragrance department has sample
  vials for testing the different colognes and per-
  fumes. Some of them are marked TESTER ONLY.
  Test each one of them—on salesclerks, shoppers,
  mannequins, and yourself. See how many different fragrances you can spray on one arm. See how
  close you can get to someone before she can smell
  you.
- **Escalator Tumbling:** Take the escalator to the next
  floor, letting your feet get caught at the end of the

ride. Tumble forward and sprawl yourself into the fine china collection. Get up and stagger back to the top of the escalator. Somersault down the steps. Stop rolling before you hit the bottom, and ride up again—this time on your back with legs draped over the handrail. When the salesclerk pries you off the steps, say you're looking for the optometry department.

- *Lights Off:* Find the store's light display and unplug it. Watch for someone to notice. If no one does, file the report yourself. When it's plugged back in, wait a few moments (go rearrange a mannequin or two), and then unplug it again.

5.

Group Dates

Admit it. Your friends think you're boring and you want to prove them wrong. This is your chapter. Try the ideas in here and see if they don't change their opinion.

Grail Hunting

After all the couples arrive at your house, you and all the other women sneak out the back door. When the men try to figure out where you went, they'll discover an envelope taped to the door. The note inside tells the men that their mission that evening is to find the Holy Grail: "And wherever your search shall lead you, you shall announce to those in your midst the purpose of your mission. You shall shout together, as with one voice, 'We are on a quest to find the Holy Grail!' and shall follow the instructions of all who give them."

An address is scribbled on the bottom of the directive. The men hop in the car and find a gas station at that address. They shout in unison at the attendant: "We are on a quest to find the Holy Grail!" After a brief fit of laughter, the attendant hands the next clue to the guys. They dash off to declare their quest to the next clue holder. After several clues—and many em-

YEAH, MY NAME
IS "GRAIL"
WHADDYA WANT,.... PUNK?

DAD

barrassing declarations—they are finally led to the
"Holy Grail," a silver cup sitting on the dining table at
one of the women's houses. The cup is filled with slips
of paper—each with a question that members of the
group take turns answering in order to get to know
one another better. A substantial meal is also on the
table to prove to the men that their quest around town
was well worth it.

—Douglas Pollock, *Knoxville, Tennessee*

Traffic Sign Acting

You'll need a camera, some costumes, and a car. Try
to find traffic signs that can be acted out. For example,
one of you can dress like a nerd and stand in front of a
DIP sign. Dress ultra-conservative and stand under
KEEP RIGHT. Smear mud on your face, chew on grass,
and crawl beneath a CATTLE CROSSING sign. Take photos
of the actors, then photograph the faces of those that
stop to watch the show.

—Chris Awalt, *Odessa, Texas*

Find Your Friends

Split your group into two teams. The members of one team try to disguise themselves with costumes and hide anywhere in a shopping mall. The second team waits 30 minutes and then goes in to find them. Those hiding may try to blend in by posing as shoppers, mannequins, security guards, drinking fountains, or hanging ferns. After everyone on the first team has been rounded up, let the second team get their costumes and give it a try.

The best disguise ever used was worn by Ernest Flimditch of El Paso, Texas. In November 1986, he entered a mall dressed as a trash can. He has not been seen since. Ernie, if you are hiding in the bookstore and can read this, go ahead and come out—you won the game fair and square.

Outdoor Restaurant

Instead of eating at a restaurant, set up your own in a vacant lot. While one couple cooks over a camp stove, another couple acts as waiters. A third couple pro-

One of the World's Worst Dates #5

January 2, 1987: Santee, California

Jack's directions got him lost en route to Stacy's house. Her phone was busy each time he stopped to call for directions, and so he was nearly an hour late when he found her house. The older man at the door greeted him warmly and invited him inside. After a few minutes of small talk, Jack asked him if his daughter was ready to go. "I don't have a daughter! Aren't you here for the Amway meeting?"

At that moment people began to arrive for the meeting, and Jack explained his mistake. He called Stacy's house again and finally got through to get better directions. Then he had to bribe his way out of the house by agreeing to purchase a year's supply of detergent.

He found Stacy's house and they drove to dinner. During the meal he went to the rest room to blow his nose. For some reason this set off a massive nose bleed, and the constant flow kept him at the sink for some time. Meanwhile, Stacy began to think she had been ditched. After

vides music and entertainment. When dinner is ready, sit down and eat the meal together. If people pass by and want to join you, tell them to take a number and start washing dishes. First they work, then they eat.

Drive-In Drama

Take your group to a drive-in theater playing a familiar movie. Park your car backward in the last row. Have each person in your group dress as a character in the movie. When the movie starts, turn on your head-

checking the parking lot for his car, she summoned a busboy to check the rest room. The busboy relayed the message that Jack was okay, and that she should start eating without him. She finished before Jack stopped bleeding, and so she had to go into the rest room to get money for the meal.

THE OUTCOME: This was their first and last date, but it had a profound effect on each of them: Stacy is now studying nursing, and Jack is the top-selling Amway distributor in his region.
—Brian C. Whiteside, *El Cajon, California*

lights for stage lighting, and act out what you see on the screen. Anybody seeing you do this will think you are idiots. They would be correct.

Positive Picket

Let's say the government decided against putting a nuclear-waste dump in your neighborhood. Or the town council finally tossed out the law prohibiting gerbils inside city limits. These are things worth celebrating! Form a picket line using signs, balloons, smiles, and laughter to convey your approval of the act. Make a party that brings attention to what you believe in.

Create a Date

Have each couple design 30 minutes of a date. Each idea can be totally unrelated to the others: tag-team wrestling on the steps of the capitol, turtle racing on the top of a billboard, solving a murder mystery in the train station, eating dinner in the trunk of a taxi.

Star for a Day

If you have friends flying in from out of town, have several couples meet them at the airport. Dress as reporters and photographers and rush them as soon as they step off the plane. Shove microphones and cameras in their faces, and interview them all the way to baggage claim. By the time they get out the door, they'll be surrounded by spectators—some of them asking for autographs. If you can, get someone to videotape the commotion. The shock of your friends and the reactions of the crowd are worth viewing again.

Date Charades

Divide your group into two teams. Go into separate rooms and have each team create a date experience that includes a fun activity, a dinner, and a dessert. After this, come back together. One member from team A goes to team B and asks what activity they have chosen. Without telling the teammates what it is, he or she must now act out this activity for team A to guess. Since they are being timed, team A wants to guess as quickly as possible: Stop the clock when they correctly guess the activity. Now reverse the roles and have one member from team B act out team A's activity. Total the times after all three parts—activity, dinner, dessert—of both groups' dates have been acted out. The team with the lower combined time gets to be treated to their original three ideas.

Bizarre Art

Get together and create pieces of contemporary art. Sculpt objects out of Play-Doh; glue cat hair to black velvet; wrap carrots in foil and poke them through a baked potato; use rotten banana peels to simulate papier-mâché and design a pie tin. Take samples of your collection to the parking lot of an art gallery. Place exorbitant prices on each object. When others ask what it is, look at them as if to say, "Are you crazy? It's art that can only be experienced."

Group Picture

Create an outrageous set: Sit in lounge chairs in the city fountain; get locked into the back of a police car; perform headstands on fire hydrants; dress as bulldozers and rev your engines in front of a new housing tract. Choose your best shot and have prints made for everyone.

—Scott Rachels, *Huntington Beach, California*

Adult Playground

Have your group invade a playground (invasion should take place after prime hours or you may bury small children in the sand). Try to remember all the games you played as a kid: get four people to form a train as you go down the slide; skip bars as you climb across the jungle gym; fall from the top of the rocket and cry for your mother; kick sand in your date's face and throw the swing into his head while he rubs his eyes and then run away as if you didn't do anything and go play with someone else's date.

Street Games

Host a series of games and competitions that your entire block can play. Feel free to try our favorites or invent your own.

- *Jacuzzi Dip:* See how long each person can stay underwater in a 105 degree hot tub.
- *Tire Iron Toss:* See how close you can come to the street sign.
- *Car Carry:* Carry everyone's car from one end of the block to the other; try to beat last year's time.
- *Branch Relay:* See how many branches you can remove from one neighbor's tree and place on another neighbor's lawn.

6.

Creative Group Dinners from A to Z

First came the *potluck* dinner—each couple brought a different food dish and shared it with the others. Since everyone kept losing Corning Ware at these gatherings, someone invented the *progressive* dinner. Each couple was responsible for one course of the meal, and since they got to serve that course in their own home they could keep an eye on their casserole dish. These dinners had their drawbacks too. Since you couldn't see what was for dessert until you arrived at the last house, you wouldn't know whether it was worthwhile to save room for it or just blow it off and take a fourth helping of three-bean salad. Then came a solution: the *regressive* dinner. It started with dessert, so if that was really good, you could go home from there and the next day tell everyone that you got lost on the way to the main course. But even those meals can get old; so we felt it was time someone came up with new and creative ways to share meals. Listed alphabetically are some of the latest meal ideas sweeping the country. Give one a try at your next opportunity—just keep an eye on your serving platter.

- *Abusive Dinner:* Take turns yelling and throwing food at each other—it looks a lot like a high school cafeteria.

- *Belching Dinner:* Instead of holding your belches until after dinner, let them fly right there at the table. Grade each other on volume, speed, duration, and smell. (Make sure to serve the right types of beverages.)
- *Camouflage Dinner:* Disguise everything to look like green peas.
- *Depressive Dinner:* Act despondent, twirling your forks in the vegetables.
- *Educational Dinner:* Have everyone prepare a short lesson on the essential vitamins contained in their contribution to the meal. Give extra credit if they know the caloric value and grams of fat in each serving.
- *Forward Dinner:* Serve people whatever you want at any time you want without asking their permission.
- *Gnashing Dinner:* Grind your teeth while eating.
- *Happy Dinner:* A new concept for many people. This is where you get along well, treat one another decently, and eat everything on your plates.
- *Intuitive Dinner:* Cover each portion of the meal and let people guess what it might be. The one who is correct may proudly say, "I *knew* it was going to be meatloaf."

- *Judgmental Dinner:* After devouring each portion of the meal, hold up cards rating it on a one-to-ten scale.
- *Knee-Jerk Dinner:* Suspend bars above the table; have everyone hang by their legs and eat the food below them. (This is best done for formal affairs when you want to avoid spilling food in your lap.)
- *Lacrosse Dinner:* A normal meal except you use lacrosse sticks instead of silverware.
- *Mitten Dinner:* Everyone wears wool mittens. No fair using silverware. Try to keep the fuzz off your teeth—it looks awful.
- *Optimistic Dinner:* Set one cracker on the table. Take turns sharing the positive contributions this cracker can make to the essence of who you are as a significant member of this dynamic society.
- *Passive Dinner:* Every time something is offered to you, politely say no thanks.
- *Quality Dinner:* Slice one top-cut steak into slivers—one for every person. Now set a 50-pound bag of dog food on the table and give a short lesson on why you believe that quality is more important than quantity.
- *Random Dinner:* Serve each section of the meal whenever you want—or not at all.
- *Seasick Dinner:* Serve seafood for every course, and cause the table to sway during the meal. When the table gets too bumpy, toss salt and water on each other.
- *Tease Dinner:* Serve a favorite dish to everyone, including the guest of honor. Just before he or she takes a bite, pull the plate away and replace it with the usual . . . tuna casserole.
- *University Dinner:* Serve frozen burritos, Top Ramen, and Coke.
- *Valedictorian Dinner:* Everything that is served must be perfect.
- *Waistline Dinner:* Measure everyone's waist be-

Dating Etiquette

Once taught to all youngsters as an essential subject, etiquette is now almost nonexistent in the curricula and behavior of young people today. The following points of etiquette are presented for the sake of the deprived who wish to become more socially graceful.

Door Manners

Despite what you see in public, it is still considered inappropriate to slam a door in your date's face.

Formal Table Manners

Always
... set down the knife before taking a bite with your fork.
... place the napkin in your lap, rather than drape it over your head.
... stay out of a food fight, unless someone else starts it.

fore and after the meal. Give dessert only to those who gain an inch or more—make the lightweights clean up.

- *Xerox Dinner:* Make photocopies of meals displayed in a gourmet food magazine, paste them onto copies of fine china, and set the table with copies of silver and crystal. Now serve macaroni and hotdogs.
- *Yard Dinner:* Serve in your back yard—out of a yard-long rain gutter.
- *Zealous Dinner:* Have a pre-meal pep rally. Now

Never
. . . squish peas between your teeth and smile at your date.
. . . greet table guests with a "high five."
. . . pour chicken gravy on the hostess's silk gown.

Strolling

When a couple is walking together along a sidewalk, it is considered proper for the man to walk nearest the street. When in a park, the woman should walk next to the man and not chase squirrels and rabbits.

Introductions

The woman is to be introduced first in any setting. When greeting a woman, a man may either shake or kiss her hand, but never lick it.

give everyone 60 seconds to eat. (Best to serve after Depressive Dinner.)

7.

I Love You in 52 Languages*

Here's how to say those powerful words differently every week for a year. You're right—some of these aren't really languages, but we ran out of foreigners to talk to. We've also included helpful words and phrases when appropriate.

Albanian

How to write it: Të dua
How to say it: të doo wa
Helpful phrase: Dëshiron të shkosh me mua tì shiko-jmë nendetësit?
(Would you like to go to the submarine races?)

Publisher's note: Fields and Temple are wholly responsible for the accuracy of this chapter. If they are as unconventional with their linguistics as they are with their dates, don't blame us.

Amazoneze

How to say it:

American Sign Language

How to say it:

Helpful phrase:

Ancient Piratese

How to say it:

HAR WENCH !

Arabic

How to write it: جبرى ·

How to say it: Bahibak

Braille

How to write it:

Helpful phrase:

(Are you sure you don't want me to drive?)

Breton

How to write it: Te a garan
How to say it: tay a garan

Catalon

How to write it: T'estimo
How to say it: tay steemoe

Cayapa (Ecuador)

How to write it: Nunu estenve
How to say it: nyou no es teng veh

Cotabato Manobo (Philippines)

How to write it: Mehidewan ku kuna
How to say it: muhiduwan koo koona

Daeron's Runes (Middle Earth)

How to write it: ᛁ ᚳᚩᚱ ᚾᛋ

Helpful phrase: ᚠᚩ ᚾᛋ ᛁᚱᚱ ᛋᛗᛏ ᛁᛗᛁ
(Do you shave your toes?)

Danish

How to write it: Jeg elsker dig
How to say it: yay elska day

Dutch

How to write it: Ik howu van jou
How to say it: ick how von yow

Early Cro-Magnon

How to say it:

Finnish

How to write it: Mina rakistan sinva
How to say it: meemay rakistan seenva

French

How to write it: Je t'aime
How to say it: zhe tem
Helpful phrase: Je regrette mais magasiner pour acheter des pneus n'est pas mon idée d'une sortie agreable.
(Sorry, but shopping for tires is not my idea of an enjoyable date.)

German

How to write it: Ich liebe dich
How to say it: eesh leebah deesh

Greek

How to write it: Σ' ἀγαπῶ
How to say it: say agapoe
Helpful phrase: Ειναι Ελληνικὰ γιὰ μὲνα.
(It's Greek to me.)

Haitian Creole

How to write it: M'rinmin ou
How to say it: m rimin ooh
Helpful phrase: Ki laj ou? Se vre!?
(How old are you? Is that right!?)

Hebrew

How to write it: ‏אני אוהבת אותך
How to say it: anee ohevet otkha

High Schoolese

How to say it:

Hungarian

How to write it: Én szerelem teged
How to say it: ayn sayrelem tayged

Italian

How to write it: Ti amo
How to say it: tee amoe

Latin

How to write it: Te amo
How to say it: tay amoe

Macedonian

How to write it: Sakan te
How to say it: sakan tay

Mayo (Mexico)

How to write it: Enchine nakke
How to say it: encheenay nakay

Mixteco (Mexico)

How to write it: Kumaniri jiinro
How to say it: kumahneeree heenrow

Morse Code (International)

How to write it:

  •• •—••   ——— •••— • —•—— ——— ••—

How to say it: dit-dit dit-dah-dit-dit dah-dah-dah
dit-dit-dit-dah dit dah-dit-dah-dah
dah-dah-dah dit-dit-dah

Helpful phrase:

—•• ——— —• •————• — —•— •• ••• ••• ——

• —••••— —•••• —— —•—— •—••• •— •—• •

—• — ••• •— •—• • •—— •— — —•—• ••••

•• —• ——• •—•—•—

      (Don't kiss me—my parents are
watching.)

Mozabite

How to write it: Chusrach wayloo
How to say it: koosrach wayloo

Mura-Piraha (Brazil)

How to write it: Tshiga ogibaai
How to say it: cheegah ohgeebah-eye

Nahuatl (Aztec)

How to write it: Ni-mitz-tlazohtla
How to say it: ni meetz clasoetcla

Norwegian

How to write it: Jeg elsker deg
How to say it: yai elskeh dai
Helpful phrase: Kan jeg få lov å synge deg en sang om hvaler?
(Would you mind if I sang you a whaling song?)

Papiamentu (Netherlands Antilles)

How to write it: Mi ta stima bo
How to say it: mee tah steemah bo

Pig Latin

How to write it: Iyay ovelay ouyay
How to say it: iyay uvlay ooyay
Helpful phrase: Ouryay Ickeymay Ousemay oelaces-shay areyay eallyray utecay.
(Your Mickey Mouse shoelaces are really cute.)

Polish

How to write it: Ja cie kocham
How to say it: ya tseh kokham

Portugese

How to write it: Eu te amo
How to say it: ayu tay amoe

Rambosa

How to say it:

Rumanian

How to write it: Ît iubesc
How to say it: it yubesk

...AND HERE'S HOW YOU SAY IT IN RUMANIAN,.....

ZZ ZZZZZ

Russian

How to write it: Я тебя люблю

How to say it: ya taybyah loobloo

Helpful phrase:

Да́йте, пожа́луйста, холо́дной осетри́ньı.

(Bring me some cold sturgeon, please.)

Semaphore

How to say it:

I   L O V E   Y O U   !

Helpful phrase:

THEY SEND LOVE LETTERS AND DO AEROBICS AT THE SAME TIME

Serbo-Croatian

How to write it: Volimte
How to say it: voleemte

Signal Flags

How to say it:

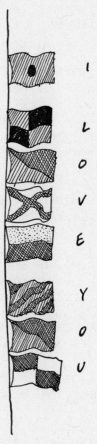

YELLOW

RED

WHITE

BLUE

BLACK

I
L
O
V
E
Y
O
U

Spanish

How to write it: Te amo
How to say it: tay amoe

Swahili

How to write it: Mimi napenda vwe
How to say it: meemee napenda vway

Swedish

How to write it: Jag alskar dig
How to say it: yag elskar day

Tagalong

How to write it: Niahal kita
How to say it: neeahal keeta

Tarahumara (Mexico)

How to write it: Nihe nimi gare
How to say it: neehay neemee gahray

Turkish

How to write it: Seni seviyorum
How to say it: saynee sayveeyorum

Vietnamese

How to write it: Tôi yêu anh (male to female); Tôi yêu
                   em (female to male)
How to say it: dtoy eeoo ahn; dtoy eeoo em
Helpful phrase: Anh cóthích nhac polka không?
                   (Do you like polka music?)

Wandamen (Indonesia)

How to write it: Isanemi vesie au
How to say it: eesahnaymee vehsee a-ow

Welsh

How to write it: Rwyi'n dy garu di
How to say it: rrwyin diygaroo dee

Zapoteco (Mexico)

How to write it: Chacda chio
How to say it: chockdah cheeyoh

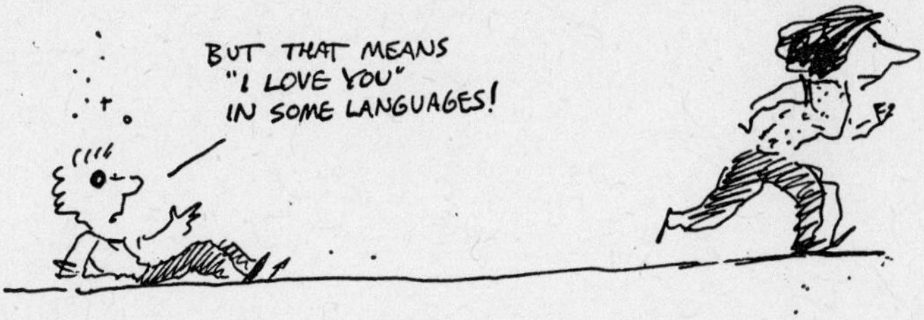
BUT THAT MEANS
"I LOVE YOU"
IN SOME LANGUAGES!

8.

Outlandish Dates

Here are some dating ideas so wild that just reading them can be perilous. If you're crazy enough to actually try one of these, it will be an experience your date will never forget.

Get Smart

You are Control Agent Maxwell Smart. While driving in your car with a date, slip off your shoe and begin talking. Yes, you'll meet Agent 31 at a phone booth on the next corner. Pull over and pick up a yo-yo from the ten-year-old dressed in a trench coat—the one standing in the booth. It's no ordinary yo-yo; it is actually a microfilm canister smuggled out of Wisconsin, and it contains the blueprints of a top-secret nuclear holstein.

At dinner, take apart the yo-yo and remove a film negative. Drip iced tea onto the film with an eyedropper, made from the bulb of a real eyedropper and the body of a retractable pen, concealed in your sock. Answer your shoe again. You are to meet Agent 56 in the alley behind the restaurant in 15 minutes. In the alley, knock on walls, talk to boxes, and question parked cars until you discover Agent 56 in a trash can when you toss some garbage into it. Slip him the film and run to your car.

When a Chaos agent grabs your date and holds a ray gun to her head, pull out a plastic toy cow and threaten to blow everyone up. Tie him up with the yo-yo string and speed away in your car. When you say good-night, insist on searching her apartment first, and then mistake the closet for the front door on your way out.

Car Fun

Some limousine services also own vintage and exotic cars that can be hired with a driver. You can build a date experience around a new Rolls Royce, an old Packard touring car, or a '56 Ford convertible. If you really want to make a statement with your dating transportation, shop around for a double-decker bus, fire truck, London cab, hearse, ambulance, or space shuttle.

If you want to do your own driving, then look for a car-rental agency that specializes in luxury automobiles. You and your friend can ride about in a Lamborghini, Jaguar, Bentley, or T-Bird.

If your budget is tight, consider renting a clunker. For as little as five dollars a day, you can get behind the wheels of some of Detroit's most hideous inventions. Start off the date by shopping for the ugliest rent-a-heap—look for obnoxious colors, tattered upholstery, serious dents. Now go out to eat at a posh restaurant. Slip the valet a five and tell him to treat it nice.

Never Alone

This date requires the help of lots of friends willing to act crazy for an evening. You're sitting at your date's house waiting for the limousine to take you to dinner. There's a honk outside, and you grab your coats and hurry to the street. What you thought was a limo turns out to be rusty pickup truck loaded with hay bales. It's being driven by a man named Earl, who is wearing overalls, a straw hat, and rubber galoshes. His brother's limousine broke down and he was asked to fill in until the problem got taken care of. You climb in only after he promises that the limousine will be fixed in time to pick you up after dinner. During the drive he insists on playing Johnny Paycheck and singing along off-key.

Dinner at the restaurant is nice, except that the couple sitting across from you keep staring at your date. When they get up to leave they ask if she is Barbara Billingsly from *Leave it to Beaver*.

After dinner you go outside to find there's no limousine in sight. And Earl isn't there either. Within moments you are greeted by a man wearing a green polyester double-knit suit and no less than twelve neckties. There's a large name tag on his lapel: "Hello, my name is Francis." He tells you he collects ties and wants yours. You politely decline until he politely pulls out a two-foot-long machete from his pant leg (your tie had a spot on it anyway). Francis leaves with your tie. Earl's wife Glenda drives up in a station wagon.

"Are you the couple waiting for the limousine?" she screams out the window. In reply to your unconvinced nod, she explains that her brother-in-law is deeply sorry for the inconvenience, but the limo is still not running and she can drop you off at the coffeehouse for dessert. The two of you climb into the back seat to discover that you're not alone—all four of the family dogs have come along for the ride.

Glenda keeps glancing into the rearview mirror and commenting on how cute you are as a couple. Then she recounts the history of her courtship, missing the off-ramp. Meanwhile, the dogs are licking your date's neck. You finally get to the coffeehouse abut halfway through Glenda and Earl's engagement, so you patiently wait through the wedding-day highlights. As you get out Glenda assures you that Earl will be at the curb within the hour.

Inside the coffeehouse all is well—the dessert wonderful and the conversation certainly not lacking—which is why it comes as such a shock to your date when she is mobbed by eight teenagers on your way out. Pictures, autographs, pieces of clothing—they want them all. You insist that she's not Amy Carter, but they don't believe you. The only thing that saves you is a tow truck driving by. In the passenger's seat is a man in a chauffeur's uniform apologizing profusely for the inconvenience. The two of you leap into the truck and hear about Pete's radiator problem all the way back to her house—a long journey made longer because the driver insists on taking his coffee break at a doughnut shop along the way.

Limousine Tips

Most of us can't afford riding this way very often, but for the rare times we are able to, a limousine can be a fantastic way to travel. The next time you get an opportunity to rent a limousine, keep in mind these simple do's and don'ts.

Do
. . . bring your own cassettes to play in the stereo.
. . . play with the intercom, telephone, stereo, tv, and electric sunroof—you paid for it.
. . . try to get the driver lost by giving the wrong directions.
. . . drive by friends' houses so you can show off
. . . pay for the service.
. . . convince the driver to do doughnuts in the parking lot.
. . . send your driver into a store while you take the limo for a spin.

Don't
. . . expect to find a bathroom on board.
. . . make your date sit in the front seat.
. . . do any off-road driving (unless it's a shortcut).
. . . carve your initials into the teakwood door panels.
. . . have more than 14 couples share in the date.
. . . stand through the sunroof when going under low bridges.
. . . rent a limousine for four hours and have it sit in a restaurant parking lot for three.

Drive-Throughs

After spending 150 dollars or more for three hours of limousine service, it's a waste to spend two of those hours dining in a schmaltzy restaurant while the driver sits in the back seat of the limousine watching *I Love Lucy* reruns on the tv. Instead of eating at the restaurant, just drive through. Have the chauffeur drive you to the entrance of an elegant restaurant (or at least to a restaurant with an elegant entrance). The doorman steps to the car and opens your door: "Good evening, sir, and welcome to The Ritz."

"Why thank you," you reply, "will you pose with us next to the car for just a moment while Jennings snaps a photo?" While you, your date, and the doorman stand for a photo, your driver (whose name is really Bert) takes a picture with your camera. As soon as the camera flashes, you slip the doorman two dollars, get back in the car, and visit the McDonald's drive-through down the street.

Don't order too much there—you'll be visiting two more drive-up windows around town to order drinks and dessert. Drive to the roof of a multistory parking structure and waltz beneath the security lights to music played over the cassette deck.

Space for Lease

Find a building with offices for lease. Call and see if you can rent one of these for a few hours. Create an intimate dining spot in the center of the 2,000-square-foot floor; throw a party with no furniture; rent studio lights and conduct a photo session; or hang backboards and play full-court basketball.

Mission Improbable

It is a Saturday morning and you, a friend, and your dates are set for an all-day excursion. As the four of you walk to your friend's car, a van pulls up to the curb. Six masked men leap out. Four of them carry you and the other man off and throw you into the van—the other two prevent the women from interfering. The van races away, leaving the women alone and bewildered. Then they notice a package dropped by one of the kidnappers.

Opening the package, they find a small tape recorder, a locker key, and two plane tickets to a nearby city. The voice on the tape tells them that if they ever want to see their dates again, they will have to be on that flight. They are advised to take the recorder and the locker key to receive their next instructions. At the airport they open the locker matching the number on the key. The cassette in the locker has more instructions that they listen to once in the air.

After their plane lands, they dial a number, letting it ring just once before hanging up. Thirty seconds later they call back. The phone call is answered by a machine, and the message instructs them to go to the gift shop near gate 5 and look on page 77 of the last *Glamour* magazine in the rack. In the magazine they find an envelope containing a Polaroid photo of a guy reading *Field and Stream*. On the back of the photo *Find this man* is written, along with a dialogue of code words.

Outside the gift shop, the two women spot a man reading *Field and Stream*—he matches the photo. They approach him and begin the dialogue written on the picture, "Fish are slippery."

Without looking up, he replies in a deadpan voice, "Fish are slimy."

The women respond, "Fish are smelly."

Without a glance, the man stands and walks away, leaving a manila envelope where he was sitting. In it is another cassette. The voice on the tape tells the women to go to parking lot "A" and look for a white Toyota sedan with a copy of *Better Homes and Gardens* on the dashboard.

They find the car unlocked, the keys tucked inside the magazine, a cassette in the tape deck. The message on this tape tells them to follow the directions on the map in the glove compartment—they lead to a grocery store. The tape also has a list of grocery items they are

to purchase when they get there. One of the items is a box of Captain Crunch cereal, but they are to take the last box on the shelf. Of course, there is another cassette taped to the back of the box.

This tape instructs them to drive to a certain park and set the bag of groceries, along with the portable cassette player, on a bench near the merry-go-round. As soon as they set down the bag, the van appears and one of the kidnappers runs to the groceries. He removes the box of Captain Crunch and the tape player and returns to the van. You and your friend are shoved out of the van as it pulls away.

This kidnapping business has left you very hungry, so you ask if the women have anything to eat. It so happens that they have a grocery bag filled with picnic supplies and are more than willing to share it with you two. There is also an envelope in the bag (left by the one who took the Captain Crunch) containing four plane tickets home that evening. Since you have the whole afternoon to kill, you drive around the town, all the while pretending that you have no idea who the kidnappers are, whose Toyota you are driving, or what city you are in. When it comes time for the flight, you notice a Hertz ID number on the front bumper, and suggest that maybe the kidnappers rented or stole the car. You let off the other three at the curb, drive to the car return, and pay for the car you had rented that morning. The others meet you at the gate where you board a flight home.

DO YOU THINK WE GOT ON THE WRONG FLIGHT?

Since you have no way home from the airport, you all catch a cab to your house. Then in your car you drive your friend and his date to her house, where his car had been left after the kidnapping. On their doorsteps that night, each woman finds a curious assortment: an album containing photos of the whole episode from the time of the kidnapping to the payoff at the park, copies of *Field and Stream* and *Better Homes and Gardens,* and a box of Captain Crunch.

Here's how you set this up: The kidnappers drive you straight to the next city—about 90 minutes away. The women's flight leaves 90 minutes after the kidnapping, so you have just enough time to drive to the other airport, set up the photograph trick, and rent the car. Then you hide the tape at the grocery store and return to the airport to pick up the *Field and Stream* reader and the photographer.

You follow the women to the grocery store for more photos, then take the photographer to the park to catch the payoff. He meets the van on the next block, and they drive back to your town to develop the film and leave the goods at the doorsteps. The phone recording is taken care of by another friend who turns his phone recorder on after he hears the first ring. He is also around to take photos at the abduction scene and again at the first airport as the women search the locker. The tapes are recorded days earlier, and the flights booked weeks beforehand.

This date is expensive and time-consuming. And since it is complicated, there are lots of things that can go wrong. Before attempting such an adventure, consider how it might backfire:

1. One of the kidnappers gets shot by a suspicious neighbor.
2. The women don't know how to turn on the tape recorder.
3. They turn it on but don't understand the tape because you mistakenly recorded the instructions in Russian.
4. They miss the plane by accident.
5. They miss the plane *on purpose.*
6. The plane crashes and you drive all the way to the next city for nothing.
7. They crash the rental car.

8. Someone buys the box of cereal before they do.
9. The kidnappers throw you out of the van—at 40 miles per hour.
10. The women leave you in the park (tied up and gagged), take the food, and go out with the two male airline attendants.

9.

Creative Gift Giving

It's not so much what you give as it is how you give it. Here are some creative and outrageous ways to give a gift.

Balloon Burial

Set your gift on a table in the middle of a room, and suspend a flashlight above it. Now fill the room with balloons, turn out the lights, and let your friend follow the light's beam to the surprise.

Please note:

1. Don't use this idea if the gift is a porcupine.
2. Don't fill the balloons with hydrogen if your friend smokes.

Friendly Doorman

Imagine this: You and your date have gotten lost trying to find a new restaurant. You pull up to the front of a hotel and your date asks the doorman for directions. He ducks inside to ask a bellman, but comes back with a wrapped gift. He gives her the gift and you the directions you need. A quick stop at the hotel on your way to pick up your date (and a five dollar tip to the helpful

HELLO, I'M DAVE THE DOORMAN, AND WITH THIS LITTLE GIFT I'D LIKE TO ASK FOR YOUR HAND IN MARRIAGE!

doorman) is all it takes to pull off this trick. Your date may never mind getting lost again.

Rainbow Chasing

Paint a rainbow on the side of his house (if it's too cold to paint, hang colored paper). Bury your gift to him at the end of the rainbow. If you can afford to be authentic, hide a pot of real gold. If you can't afford that, just fill up a small saucepan.

Delivery Alternatives

Parcel companies like UPS and Federal Express aren't the only delivery services in town. A taxicab will drop something off for the price of the fare. Tip the diaper man to deliver a gift wrapped in diapers (request clean ones). If the gift is small enough, the bottled-water man can stuff it in an empty bottle. With the right contacts, a little begging, and some nice tips,

you can have your gifts delivered by plumbers, exterminators, paperboys, and cookie-hawking Girl Scouts.

Birthday Locker

Go to an airport, bus station, or shopping mall and fill a locker with all the essentials for a birthday surprise. Go get the birthday girl, give her the key, and follow her to the locker. When she opens the door, helium balloons float out and a banner taped to the inside of the door falls open. There are flowers in a vase, a cake with candles waiting to be lit, and lots of little gifts hidden amongst the crepe paper and streamers that fill the locker. If the locker will fit them, hire a children's choir to start singing as soon as she opens the door.

—Pamela Courts, *Batavia, Ohio*

Delayed Reaction

Hide a gift that your friend won't find until days or weeks later. Conceal it in the lawn mower bag, under the sewing machine in the closet in the spare room, or inside a hubcap on his car. If some day you find him elated for no apparent reason, you can guess that he fixed the rattle in his car by finding the golf balls you had forgotten.

Prize Inside

Remove the contents of a cake-mix box, hide a small gift inside, then put some of the mix back in to cover it up. As the two of you make a cake together, she'll find the strange clump in the ingredients. If she happens to miss it when it pours out of the container, she's sure to notice it when it causes her electric mixer to seize up.

Planned Drops

Schedule outlandish gift deliveries to take place during a date. While having dinner in the middle of a strawberry patch, a crop duster flies overhead and drops a gift that parachutes into your date's arms (this may take some practice). During a picnic in a drainage ditch, a gift floats by on the deck of a balsa-wood boat. When drinking orange juice in the middle of a boulevard, the trash truck honks, then tosses an unbreakable gift into the middle of the street. Your date will think your connections are diverse when everything that happens is of no surprise to you.

Birthday Box

If you can't be with a person on his birthday, create a party in a box and mail it to him. Fill it with streamers, balloons, confetti, party hats, noisemakers, pennies, small animals, candles, cookies, a tiered

cupcake, glass of punch, whipped cream, maraschino cherries, and a recording of Sheriff John singing "Put Another Candle on the Birthday Cake." Before mailing, throw the box against the wall to see that it is all packed securely.

—Leslie Young, *Alta Loma, California*

Giving Yourself Away

You'll need two friends, a truck, a handcart, and a box big enough for you to crawl into. Poke holes in the box so you can breathe from inside, and use stencils to paint instructions on the outside. They can say something like, ACME NURSERY . . . LIVE PLANT INSIDE—OPEN IMMEDIATELY. Climb inside and have your friends deliver you to the lucky person's door. When he opens the lid, leap out with a rose in your teeth and bouquet in your arms (if you're still breathing by the time he gets around to opening the box).

As with all harebrained ideas, there are a few cautions:

1. Visit the rest room *before* climbing in the box.
2. Ask your delivery friends to lower you from the truck *gently*.
3. See that they observe the THIS SIDE UP warning on the box.
4. Make sure they leave you at the right house.
6. Have your delivery friends warn the recipient against opening you with a knife.
7. Remove thorns from the rose before placing it in your teeth.

Giving Flowers

People don't get tired of getting flowers—but they do tire of receiving them in the same old way. Here are some new ideas.

Pet Gifts

Someone you love can experience real joy (possibly for the first time) in a relationship with one of the animals listed below.

Dogs   Almost any dog will do, but avoid one if it looks like a rat in a dog suit.

Cats   Another good choice, unless your friend has pet mice. Your gift will be even more special if you can train the cat to swim, fetch, and catch a frisbee.

Wildflowers

Gather an armful of wildflowers and greenery from a field. Be careful to avoid such varieties as poison oak, poison ivy, and stinging nettles—this is especially critical if your date is one of those who likes to bury her face in a fresh bouquet. Before giving the bundle,

Birds	Favorite varieties: canaries, parakeets, finches. Birds *not* to give: crows, pelicans, emus, buzzards.
Rodents	These make wonderful anonymous gifts: let loose in a home, they'll be a delightful surprise when discovered. They can be purchased at bulk rates from wholesale pet stores.
Cows	Beautiful animals—and healthy for lawns.
Snakes	Quiet and affectionate.
Coyotes	Intelligent, good for keeping cats out of the sandbox.
Fish	Stay away from noisy breeds; deliver in water.
Rabbits	Dead or alive? People seem divided on the issue—if you aren't sure what your friend will prefer, get a live one and he can decide for himself.
Spiders	Easy to train and feed; good company on lonely nights.
Penguins	Cute, friendly, and wonderful with children.

make every effort to remove insects, reptiles, and small rodents that have taken refuge in the foliage.

Flower Trail

Hide a gift in your date's house and lay down a trail of flowers that will lead her to it. She comes home and finds a flower in the driveway and three others leading up the walk to the porch. She discovers another leaning on the screen door and two more inside the entryway. A winding trail of blossoms leads her through virtually every room in the house before taking her to the gift.

Shredded Flowers

Run three dozen daisies through a paper shredder and deliver the bouquet in a trash bag. Tell her your dog ate it.

Flower Room

Decorate her bathroom with a hundred dollars' worth of flowers. Arrange a dozen roses in the toilet bowl and fill the tank with irises. Float gardenia blossoms in the sink and water lilies in the bath; hang orchids in the shower. Spill baby's breath and maidenhair fern from the drawers, and place a tulip in each bottle of shampoo. Don't touch the toilet paper.

10.

Holiday Dates

Celebrate this year's holidays with dates created for the occasion. After trying one of these ideas, you may need another holiday just to recover.

St. Valentine's Day

Design a date using the St. Valentine's Day massacre as your theme. Dress as gangsters, talk in a hoarse voice, and carry violin cases. Use squirt guns on anyone that laughs.

President's Day

Run for the office of her heart. Come up with campaign slogans, stickers, and posters: "You're number one with me," "I'll do what I can to make you happy," "I'm your man!" Make her attend a speech with promises of all the things you'll do for her if you are elected.

When she signs in at your voting booth, give her a ballot with a list of dating ideas that she can choose from. When you've been elected—good politicians think positive—take her on your inaugural date. Upon leaving, wave to the crowd, dodge reporters, and ignore questions dealing with foreign affairs.

May Day

Fill wicker baskets with flowers and decorate them with ribbons. On the morning of the first, drive around and leave them on the doorsteps of friends and family. Other things to put in a May Day basket: candy, soaps, candles, garden seeds, iguanas.

Fourth of July

Go on a patriotic car rally with a few other couples. Every clue should mention something associated with the colonies or the Revolutionary War. Begin at George Washington High School, buy a flag at Delaware Hardware, march down Boston Avenue, and dump tea in the fountain at Columbia Savings and Loan. The last couple to finish must memorize the

Declaration of Independence—or smoke cigars in a fireworks stand.

Halloween

A Styrofoam wig holder can make a frightful invitation to a Halloween date. To create a face for the synthetic head, use meatballs as eyes and spaghetti for hair. A cut carrot can make the nose, and bright lipstick and blush will complete the facial features. Pin the date invitation to the neck and set the head among the clutter in his closet. The next time he ventures into the closet he'll encounter your request—and immediately figure out how he can scare you to death with a reply. If he never talks to you again, then assume you triggered a nightmare that he now associates with your face.

Thanksgiving

If you don't want to cook on this holiday, go to the local fast-food restaurants and purchase the equivalent foods. Get french fries instead of baked potatoes. Throw tomatoes against the wall and step on them to create yams. Buy fried chicken and peel the skin off to take the place of your turkey. Melt raspberry sherbet for your cranberry sauce. Dip a brownie in mustard to create your own pumpkin pie.

When You're on a Date but Wish You Weren't

- Eat cheese puffs until your fingers turn yellow and your teeth turn orange.
- Feign a heart attack.
- Play dead.
- Crash the car and tell the ambulance driver to take you home alone.
- See if you can touch your tongue to your nose.
- Ask if she has any wallet photos of cute girlfriends.
- Do your nails.
- Clean your ears.

- Go to a congested area and get lost in the crowd.
- Start to drool.
- Let your wig fall off.
- Give yourself the hiccups.
- Sneeze every time he comes near you.

Christmas

Become one of Santa's helpers. Record a date invitation on a variable-speed tape recorder—use the slow setting. When she plays the tape at normal speed, you'll sound like an elf whose green stretch pants are too tight.

Here's how to deliver the tape recorder:

1. Throw it down the chimney.
2. Steal the tree and leave the recorder in its place.
3. Put it in a stocking that swings into the doorway when the door is opened.
4. Bake it into a loaf of bread.

...HOW 'BOUT DINNER AND A SHOW?

11.

Breaking Up

It's lots of fun when you start to date someone, but the fun sometimes has a catch to it: sooner or later you may want to *stop* dating that person. And stopping is much messier than starting. Maybe it's our fault that you're in this mess. You used one of our ideas to ask this person out, and together you've tested a few of our date ideas. Now you've spent plenty of quality time with this special person, and you've discovered that it's time to move on. Of course it's not *really* our fault; we never guaranteed your chances for the future. But, far be it from us to leave you without a creative idea or two to get yourself out of this spot.

In this chapter you'll find some helpful hints

I CAN'T DATE YOU ANYMORE, RICH,...
YOU'RE A...... ...YOU'RE A LIZARD.

I WONDERED WHEN YOU'D NOTICE.

wedged in among some not-so-helpful ideas. (After all, this is a *humor* book—and we won't get paid if we get too serious.)

When to Break Up

Deciding whether to break up is a difficult task, made tougher because we are emotional beings who sometimes mistake something harmless for something dangerous. The following chart can help you judge which is which.

Harmless *(don't break up)*	Dangerous *(break up)*
He helps you out of the car; you break a fingernail.	He helps you out of the car when it's going 60 mph; you break an arm, a leg, and a collarbone.
He shows up for a date and his outfit clashes with your dress.	He shows up for a date and his dress clashes with your outfit.
She accidentally spills a glass of ice water in your lap and gives you some napkins to dry yourself off.	She accidentally spills a glass of aviation fuel in your lap and offers to dry you off with a lighter.
He slips up and calls you Laura, his old girlfriend.	He slips up and calls you Laura, the flirtatious friend who has been avoiding your lately.
His bookshelves contain a copy of *Macraméing for Fun and Profit.*	His bookshelves contain a copy of *Millionaire Mercenary.*

Some other situations also warrant a breakup. If you are in one of the following circumstances, it's time to take action:

1. He says to you: "Oh Sally, Sally, Sally, you're the only woman I've ever loved"—and your name is Rebecca.
2. She sends you a postcard from the Bahamas, signed by her and someone named Bif.
3. She borrows your car for a business trip, and you see it on tv during coverage of a demolition derby.
4. You run into him at the supermarket—with his wife and kids.
5. You never have time to see him because you're too busy doing his laundry, running his errands, and cooking his meals (and you're not even married).

6. Every time you come home from a date with him, you notice money missing from your purse.
7. You're the fourth multimillionaire she has been involved with in the last five years—and the only one who still has his money.

8. His favorite historical figure is Henry VIII.
9. She says she loves you more than her seven other boyfriends—and proves it by dumping four of them.
10. You work in an embassy, you're dating a woman named Natasha, and you discover that her hobbies include photography, microelectronics, and pistols.

How to Break Up

Don't judge the quality of your relationship by one date, one weekend, or one week. The guy may have been reading *someone else's* dating book and attempted a date idea that was foreordained to be catastrophic. The quality of your relationship ought to be judged over the long haul—but if he fumbles two dates in a row, dump him.

Don't put things off. She already knows there's something wrong with the relationship because you break into hysterics each time she calls; she's perceptive—and waiting for the other shoe to drop.

Don't blame it on him. Without lying, take as much responsibility for your decision as you can. (And if you're a guilt magnet anyway, you're good at accepting *anybody's* blame already; just pile it on yourself—go ahead, you deserve it.) Heaping the blame on him may make him defensive (have him leave his scimitar outside if you do), and he may decide that losing a girlfriend is enough for one day without the added pain of losing his self-respect.

Don't declare your desire to be "just friends." Those two words are contradictory (like "just a unicorn" or "just a billion dollars"), and you cheapen the idea of friendship by connecting them. Instead, try an expression like "just pals," "just chums," "just buddies for life," or "just fellow members of the same socioeconomic group."

If you break up, break up. Don't confuse him by calling only when you're lonely, bored, or need to have your ego (or a flat tire, for that matter) reinflated. If those are the only times you miss him, then breaking up was exactly what the two of you needed. The only time you should ask him out again is if it's *really* important: your lawn needs mowing or your mother has set you up with the curator of a bottle-cap museum.

Where to Break Up

"Location, location, location" is the first phrase real estate agents learn to recite in school. While choosing the wrong location when buying real estate can cost you money, choosing a poor location when telling someone you're breaking up can cost you your health. While no location can take away the tension that such a conversation produces, many locations can make a

bad situation worse. Through extensive research, we have determined the ten worst places to say to someone, "I want to break up":

1. Halfway across a tall bridge.
2. In the middle of a karate class.
3. The center divider of an expressway while changing a tire.
4. Any remote jungle, forest, or swampland.
5. In the cutlery section of a department store.
6. In the large mammal area of a zoo.
7. In a plane taking the two of you up for a parachute jump.
8. At a riflery range.
9. Within view of the admissions office of a mental hospital.
10. In a cemetery.

Breaking Up Exam

Test your breaking-up skills by taking this short exam:

1. You're sitting at dinner with your date. Suddenly your lap feels cold and wet, and the unmistakable smell of aviation fuel fills the air. Your date has a curious smile on her face, and an ignited lighter in her hand. To ease the tension of the moment, you toss off a joke: "No thanks, I don't smoke—except when I'm on fire." She replies, "Let's find out." What conclusions can you draw regarding your relationship with this woman?

a. *She doesn't know that your mother buys you flameproof underwear.*
b. *Her requesting the smoking section of the restaurant was no accident.*
c. *She's not as fond of you as you had assumed.*
d. *It's probably a good time to draw the curtain on the relationship.*
e. *All of the above.*

2. The first time it happened, you didn't let it bother you—it's easy to get a name mixed up. But in the past month he has gotten your name mixed up with someone else's on thirteen different occasions. And after all, your name is Antoinette, which doesn't really sound at all like Lila, Joan, Kim, Marsha, Shari, Anita, Mary, Judy, Wendy, Heather, Cheryl, Julia, or Marguerite. So today you have confronted him by asking, "Tom, what's my name?" A look of horror spreads across his face, but it disappears in an instant as a name lands on his tongue: "Ruth." The next move is yours . . .

a. *You reply, "Yes it's Ruth." (You like that name better anyway.)*
b. *You ask him if he would like to enroll in a memory class.*
c. *You say, "No, Bill, I'm Kim."*
d. *You tell him that you're suffering from a multiple-personality disorder and request that he leave each one of you alone.*

3. Imagine that you are about to break up with Ralph, and that you must use one of the following to do so. From what you've learned above, which approach would you use?

a. "I'm a perfect angel, and you're an obnoxious and insensitive oaf—I say we call it quits."

b. "Um ... I was ... well ... kinda thinking that ... well you know, um, you and me ... well, the thing is ... how can I put this ... oh, never mind. Where would you like to go tonight, Ralph darling?"

c. "Lunch on a traffic median?! Where in *&^%$#@!! did you get such a warped idea for a date?! I pity your next victim!"

d. "I'm no good for you Ralph. You are a butterfly, I am a worm; you are a noble prince, I am a night clerk at Otis Stadenko's Quality Books and Chicken Take Out; you deserve much better, I deserve someone closer to my own low stature—like Otis, who will be here in a few minutes to pick me up. So if you don't mind, I've got to get ready."

e. *"Listen to me, Ralphy. I'm calling to confess something I feel rotten about: the only times I want to see you are when I've been stood up by someone else. Like tonight, the most gorgeous hunk of a man—oh, just thinking of him overwhelms me so I can't even see straight—has left me here all alone. I suppose if I didn't care about you, it wouldn't hurt me to know that I use you. But I do care about you, Ralphy, and it does hurt, and the only way I'll feel better is by apologizing for my selfish behavior. And I'd feel much better if I could give you my apology in person. Could you buy me dinner?"*

4. You've decided that today is the day you're going to break the news to your girlfriend: you want out of the relationship. You've felt all along that somehow you weren't compatible. She's 6'2", you're 5'6½" with lifts; she's a professional motorcycle racer, you sell shoes

at K-Mart; she has a complete collection of The Doors albums, you prefer the Bee Gees and Sandi Patti. She's always said she'd do something drastic if you ever tried to leave her, and based on her behavior on the racetrack, you have no reason to doubt her. You've already decided *what* to tell her—now you've got to pick the location. Choose one:

a. *The exact center of the Golden Gate Bridge, in the fog, at three in the morning.*
b. *At today's motorcycle race, immediately after she loses.*
c. *At tonight's professional wrestling match, right before she introduces you to her brother, Mitch the Mauler.*
d. *In her garage, while she's welding together the pieces you're holding.*
e. *None of the above. You've decided it's about time you took that trip to visit your Aunt Edna, the one who's a missionary in Malaysia.*

For correct answers, see page 159.

12.

Pre-Date Checklist

Special dates call for special preparation. This list is designed to help you remember the countless steps you must go through to make the date come off right.

☐ Take a shower.
☐ While showering, rehearse your final lines at the doorstep: "Thanks, [insert name], I had a wonderful time. When can I see you again?"

☐ Shampoo your hair.

☐ Dry off.

☐ Climb back in the shower and rinse the shampoo out of your hair.

☐ Dry off again.

☐ Get back in the shower and lather up with the soap you forgot the first time.

☐ Get out, try to dry off with your wet towel, then streak to the linen closet to get a fresh one.

☐ On the way back to the bathroom, answer the phone, and stand there naked until you get a word in to tell the salesman peddling reverse-osmosis water purifiers that you can't talk now but will agree to a free home demonstration if he can please let you stop dripping water on your Persian rug.

☐ Go back in the bathroom and dry off. If you're male, shave. (If you're female, get in the shower again and shave this time.)

☐ Get some clothes on before the phone rings again.

☐ Take your clothes off and put on some deodorant.

☐ If you're male, wash the rest of the shaving cream off your face and find a new shirt: the first one has fresh bloodstains on the collar from the shaving nick under your chin. If you're female, wrap your wet hair in the towel so it won't soak the new top like it did the one you just took off.

☐ While blow-drying your hair, calculate the elapsed time you and your date will spend in the car. Now add up the times of the various songs on your favorite cassette album and determine exactly where to start the tape so that the romantic song starts playing just as you are driving your date home.

☐ Brush your teeth.

☐ Floss your teeth.

☐ Brush again.

☐ Change your shirt again—pick one without toothpaste splatter on the front.

☐ If you're female, put on your makeup. If you're

male, do some flexing and sparring in front of the mirror to swell up your muscles and your nerve.

☐ If you're paying for the meal tonight, run to the kitchen and make some toast to snack on so you won't be tempted to order more food than you can pay for. If you're being treated to a meal tonight, run to the kitchen and make yourself some toast to snack on so you won't be so hungry you inhale your meal.

☐ While the bread is toasting, rewind the cassette to the spot you determined earlier.

☐ When you smell the toast burning, leave the cassette player on rewind and run back to the kitchen. Throw out the cinders and load two more pieces of bread.

☐ Go back to the cassette player and fast forward the tape until you get to the correct spot. Remember the toast and put the tape in your cassette case. (Uh oh,

was that your roommate's *Fluent Flemish* language tape?)

☐ Eject the toast before it reaches the flash point and get the jelly out of the refrigerator.

☐ Change your slacks—the pair you're wearing has a ring of jelly where the jar landed when it slipped free from the loosened top.

☐ Finish preparing and eating your toast. Put away the mess, taking care not to wipe jelly on your slacks.

☐ Change slacks again—you wiped jelly on the pair you were wearing.

☐ Brush teeth again.

☐ Floss again.

☐ Brush again.

☐ Change your shirt again—the one you were wearing seems to have toothpaste splatter on it too.

☐ Work on your hair again. It dried funny—it puffs out on the sides and makes your head look three inches wider than normal.

☐ Clean out your ears with a cotton swab.

☐ Put on some cologne. Sniff the air to be sure that the smell of cologne overpowers the smell of your deodorant.

☐ It doesn't—put on more cologne.

- [ ] Look at your watch. It *must* be running 15 minutes fast—it can't be that late.
- [ ] Call time on the phone. If your date answers the phone, you dialed the wrong number. Hang up without saying anything.
- [ ] Dial time again and try to figure out whether your date could tell it was you. Hang up without checking your watch.
- [ ] Go back to the bathroom, but forget you already put on cologne. Put it on again. Now you remember.
- [ ] Wipe off as much cologne as you can and smell yourself. There's still too much. Wipe furiously. People will be able to detect the scent from you a furlong away—upwind.
- [ ] Get the bottle of rubbing alcohol from beneath the sink, soak a towel with the contents, and rub vigorously to remove the cologne. While rubbing, try to guess why your date sounded so cold and abrupt

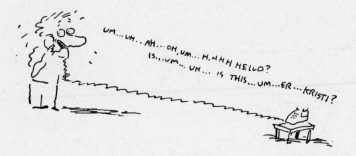

UM...UM...AH...OH, UM...H.HHH HELLO?
IS...UM... UM... IS THIS...UM...ER...KRISTI?

when answering the phone. You try to recall ever hearing a colder "Hello?" in your life. *Why is my date in such a bad mood? Maybe it's from the thought of going out with me? Oh how did I ever set myself up for this. My date probably hates me*——

☐ Hold that thought—your soon-to-be-ex roommate put the Pine Sol disinfectant in an empty rubbing alcohol bottle.

☐ Scream uncontrollably for several seconds.

☐ Stop screaming when you detect the phone ringing. Go answer it.

☐ It's your date. Think the worst: *Calling to cancel—I knew my date couldn't go through with it. I wouldn't want to go out with someone like me either, especially if I hated the person. It's probably better that*—— It occurs to you that your date is saying something to you, so you listen: "Hello? Are you there? Oh there you are. I feel silly telling you this, but I'm going to be a little . . . well . . . actually . . . about an hour late tonight. I've been really looking forward to this date, and . . . well . . . all the anticipation and nervousness has got me running around and making a fool of myself. The truth is, I kind of spilled stuff on my clothes and I'm waiting for them to dry. Is it okay with you if we run a little late?"

☐ Answer your date: "Well that's fine with me—I'm

actually running a little behind myself. I'll see you in an hour."

☐ Now start (again) at the top of this checklist, and see if you can get through the essentials in the next hour without messing up. (While you're in the shower this time, think about how special this night must be for your date, who is probably so in love with you that, well, it can't be helped when you're as stunning as you are. . . .

13.

Answers to the 25 Questions the Authors Receive Most Often About Dating

1. I've always been fascinated by pirate stories and fantasize about going on a date with a pirate someday—is there something wrong with me?

Yes.

2. Most of your dates are too wild for me. Do you have any ideas for people who are timid?

Yes, of course. Here are some ideas just for you:
• Go for a walk.
• Wax the kitchen floor.
• Read the newspaper together.
• Hold hands (briefly).
• Sit on a bench.
• Look at birds.

WELL TRISHA, THEY SAID THAT TAKING A WALK WAS A MILD DATE.

3. Is it okay to kiss on the first date?

Who is it that you want to be kissing on that date? Your parents? Yes. Your kid brother? Yes. The doorman at the restaurant? No. The waiter? No. The man who sold you popcorn at the movie? No again. The policeman, your date's roommate, the woman sitting next to you in the theater, the lamppost, the manhole cover? All no. Your date? It depends. If you have a question about it, go ahead and ask him or her. (Politeness is still respected by many as a noble virtue.)

4. How do I say no to someone who asks me out?

- "No thanks, I don't date losers."
- "I can't—thank goodness I'm busy doing something enjoyable that day."
- "Ha ha ha ha ha . . ."

5. How do I say no *without being rude?*

- "I'm getting married."
- "I'm off to another planet that weekend, sorry."

- "I'll be visiting my great grandchildren that day."
- "Let me check my calendar . . . let's see . . . darn! . . . I thought so . . . no can do—that's the weekend I begin serving my prison sentence."

6. How do I say no *without being rude OR lying about it?*

- No, thank you—I'd rather not. (You don't owe anybody a reason.)

7. How do men feel about being asked out by a woman?

Most guys are honored (they want you to ask); a few find it uncomfortable (they *need* you to ask).

8. Seriously, do you have any ideas on how I can create a date experience using a pirate theme?

Look, lady, you're nuts, and we're not about to fan the flames of your warped fantasy.

9. How do I avoid the awkwardness of a first date?

There are three ways: (1) don't date; (2) only date those you've been out with before; or (3) try the following trick.

Any time you're alone with someone you don't know, it's awkward. In the first few minutes you're together on a first date, talk about it: "Look, I feel awkward because I don't know you, and you don't know me. Let's spend the next few minutes interviewing each other so we can get over this strangeness as quickly as possible."

After you've found out the basics on each other, try this: "What if we were to say that right now is the end of our first date. Knowing what I do about you so far, I'd like to ask you out again: would you go out with me on a second date? Okay, then the second date starts now, and since we already know each other from the first date, we can forget about the awkwardness and have a good time together!"

If you are turned down for the "second" date, then the night is still young: take your date home and go out on your own. (The inventor of this technique, John Hall, once got a whole semester's worth of dating out of the way in just one night.)

10. Why do they call it necking?

We can't think of any logical reason either.

11. I always have a tough time deciding what [among the dozens of brilliant, witty, and delightful ideas in your books] to try for a date. Any ideas?

Try writing each possibility on an index card: shuffle the cards and deal one. Or have your date pick a number; flip to that page number in this book, and try the date that appears on that page. (If you land in the "Breaking Up" section, pick again; if you land three times in a row, consider it a sign.)

12. Should I expect romance on the first date?

Thank you, Mr. Klankenhorn, for sending us your photo and biographical sketch along with your question. In short: no.

13. What's a good date idea for folks who live in Cut Bank, Montana?

After a nice meal at The Ranch in Ethridge, take a drive back to the airport in town. Drive around the old buildings there until you find the dog pound; go around back to visit the dog cages. Take out the table scraps the cook at the restaurant gave you and give the dogs a nice dinner. (Careful, these dogs sometimes get confused as to what's a table scrap and what's a hand.)

Now head down to Pizza Hut with your own pint of ice cream, order a pitcher of root beer, and make yourselves a jumbo float. (Slip a green chile from the salad bar into your date's glass—see how long it takes before it's discovered.)

After dessert, swing by the Glacier Hotel and buy a postcard from the front desk. Now drive by Hegle's Auto and try to trade your postcard for a Hegle car sponge—it's a collector's item in some parts of the country.

YOU MAY BE HANDSOME, DRIVE A NEAT CAR, AND BE A JOCK, BUT YOU KNOW SOMETHING TODD? ...YOU'RE A DUD.

14. What do girls look for in guys?

Good looks, fast cars, lots of money. [When we get questions like these, we can't help but wonder—if they're not teaching basic facts like this in the schools today, what *are* they teaching?]

15. How do I say no to someone who's pressuring me to have sex?

- "I do have principles, you know; I'm against anything that causes windows to steam up."
- "If we go any further, a strange thing will happen to me: I'll feel guilty. And when I feel guilty, I become miserable, and then I make others miserable. Let's stop here—I'll feel good about myself, and I won't make you feel miserable."
- "We'd better stop here. The last time I got this close to a guy, my father shot him and had him mounted in our den. And I didn't even think he was that good looking."

- "I'm horrible at decisions when I'm breathing hard—let's talk about it later."
- "A while ago I made some decisions on what I felt were good guidelines for me in a relationship, and I decided to draw a line here. Excuse me while I go get my marking pen."
- "No."

16. But what if he doesn't seem to get the message?

- "Touch me again and you're dead meat."
  Scream very loud into his ear: "DIDN'T YOU HEAR ME?!—I SAID NO!"
- Bite his lips off.
- Call in your pet wolves.

17. There's nobody in my community for me to date—they're either married, too old, too young, or not my type. What do I do?

- Become a nun.
- Move.
- Date someone who's not your type.
- Go away, meet someone nice, and bribe him into moving to your community.
- Start up a small business that grows into a Fortune 500 company overnight, attracting hundreds of eligible young executives to your community.

18. What should I do if I'm at a restaurant, the check comes, and I don't have enough money to pay for it?

Use a credit card.

19. They don't accept plastic.

Then write a check.

20. They won't take a check, either.

Then leave your wallet with them, go home for some cash, and return to pay the tab.

21. But———

Don't tell us—we'll guess: you left your wallet at home, there's no cash in the house, and you couldn't get there anyway because your car was stolen by the parking valet and your date, who are driving all night to elope in Halifax, Nova Scotia. Look, dipstick, we've got serious questions to answer here—now leave us alone so we can minister to the needs of those with sincere problems.

22. Is there some significance in the way I turn my head while kissing?

Yes. If you turn it to the left or right, you're normal. If you don't turn at all, then you both have extremely small noses, and very likely, bruised foreheads. If you turn your head completely around during kissing, you're possessed.

23. How far in advance should I ask someone out?

There are two ways to arrive at the answer. The first is based on a simple formula that uses three factors: *Interest* (how interested you are in this person on a scale of 1 to 10, 10 being the highest); *Dates* (the number of dates you've been on together); and *Cost* (how much money you plan to spend on the date, in dollars). The equation returns a value *A*, which is equal to the number of days in advance you ought to do your asking. Here's the formula:

$$\frac{(Interest \times 100)}{Dates} + \frac{Cost}{\left(\frac{Dates^2}{Interest}\right)} \times [Cost \times (Dates + 30) - Interest] = A$$

HEY TAMMY! YOU'RE ALWAYS BUSY, SO I LOOKED UP JULY 1ST, 1989, IT'S A FRIDAY!

Or, if you're not a math genius (we aren't math genii, as you can tell), then just ask the person as soon as you can.

24. What should I wear on a first date?

There is no hard and fast rule on this; so much depends on your personal style. If you have no style, then we suggest you dress in this way:

Women: Pink paisley polyester slacks

Green, long-sleeved, turtleneck sweater

Three-inch platform sandals with naugahyde straps

Wide, black vinyl belt with orange acrylic buckle

Beehive hairdo

Jewelry and purse of your choosing

Men: Same as above (except jewelry and purse, of course)

25. Just one little pirate idea?

Okay. Have you and your date dress like pirates—old clothes, colorful scarves, lots of gold jewelry. Get in a boat, and row around the harbor until you find a large yacht with a party taking place on board. Sneak onto the boat and force everyone on board to get into the lifeboats and paddle to shore. If any resist, say things like, "Dead men tell no tales!" and "Over the side or we'll keelhaul ye, ye scurvy dogs!" When all the passengers have disembarked, run the skull and crossbones up the halyard, then sit down and finish their food and drinks. Now rehearse what you'll say to the coast guard, whose cutter is closing in at three points abaft your port beam.